# ARTYFACTS

## hal evans

BROWN BOOKS KIDS

*ArtyFacts*

Brown Books Kids
16250 Knoll Trail Drive, Suite 205
Dallas, Texas 75248
www.BrownBooksKids.com
(972) 381-0009

A New Era in Publishing®

Publisher's Cataloging-In-Publication Data

Names: Evans, Hal (Harold E.), author.
Title: ArtyFacts / hal evans.
Other Titles: Arty facts
Description: Dallas, Texas : Brown Books Kids, [2021] | Interest age level: 006-010. | Summary: "Explore some of the most iconic and famous artworks—from the Mona Lisa to the Sistine Chapel—with a new spark of fun as you sing along to the whimsical and informative songs written by hal evans!"--Provided by publisher.
Identifiers: ISBN 9781612545004
Subjects: LCSH: Art appreciation--Songs and music--Texts--Juvenile literature. | Masterpiece, Artistic--Songs and music--Texts--Juvenile literature. | CYAC: Art appreciation--Songs and music--Texts. | Masterpiece, Artistic--Songs and music--Texts. | LCGFT: Poetry.
Classification: LCC N7440 .E93 2021 | DDC [E] 701.1--dc23

ISBN 978-1-61254-500-4
LCCN 2020924465

Printed in Canada
10 9 8 7 6 5 4 3 2 1

For more information or to contact the author, please go to
www.halevanspoet.com.

# DEDICATION

*For the artists and museums who curate our humanity.*

# ACKNOWLEDGMENTS

I acknowledge with appreciation the support and guidance of Thomas Reale in bringing this book into being. His team, Samantha, Hallie, Kat, and all at Brown Books Publishing Group, made this process a creative celebration.

If a picture's worth a thousand words,
 then what is one word's worth?
We see a thing and need a word
 to give that thought its berth.

Image or imagining:
 Which plays the greater part?
Framed by their own boundlessness,
 hearts mete their terms of art.

Truth is beauty, beauty truth—
 whether it's viewed or it's versed.
These odes are owed to art that's earned
 its place and plaudits first.

*Woman in Hat and Fur Collar*, Pablo Picasso

Ol' Picasso painted form:
ear, eye, ear, eye, nose!
A face that looks two ways at once—
Knee! Thigh! Backside? . . . TOES!
    With an eyeball here
    and an elbow there,
    here a shin,
    there a chin,
    everywhere a thin grin!
Ol' Picasso painted form:
ear, eye, ear, eye, nose.

# Dauntless

sung to "Frere Jacques"

Frida Kahlo,
Frida Kahlo
painted true
what she knew.
Hearts connect to flowers,
feel the magic hours
she imparts.
Open hearts!

Frida Kahlo
lived with sorrow—
home of blue,
Casa Azul.
Her undaunted spirit
conquered every fear it
overcame.
Speak her name.

Frida Kahlo,
Frida Kahlo!

*The Frame*, Frida Kahlo

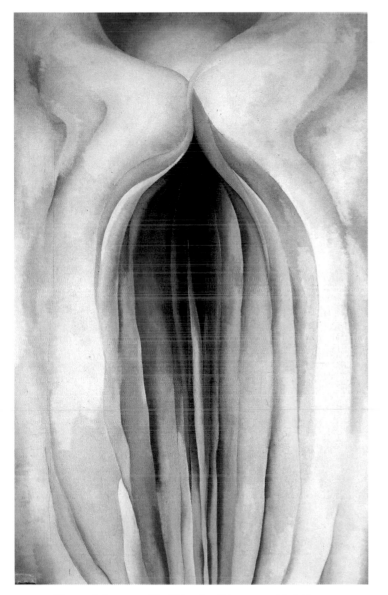

*Grey Lines with Black, Blue and Yellow,*
Georgia O'Keeffe

Shells in landscapes, Georgia O'
spied flowers in old New Mexico . . .
A cow skull . . .

Inside a wishbone she could find
a faded rainbow realigned
so beautifully.

Somewhere inside a cow skull, beauty lies.
Wishbones contain a rainbow
painted within gray lines.

Somewhere inside a cow skull through her eyes,
you'll see beauty and know what
Georgia had on her mind.

# First Impression

Claude Monet,
Claude Monet,
painted without his eyeglasses.

Near-sighted,
Claude Monet
painted a *Path through the Irises.*

Seasons change how daylight plays
on floral hazes dancing.

Claude Monet
saw the light,
captured it onto his canvasses.

*The Path through the Irises*, Claude Monet

*American Gothic*, Grant Wood

Behold the farming man.
He tends the sprawling land.
He is plain American,
a trident in his hand.

Seeds are what he'll sow,
and hay is what he'll throw.
(A trident sounds more glamorous
than "pitchfork," don't you know.)

A window to a spire
says hopes are reaching higher.
Fun, I grant, would be deserved
whenever they retire.

They're polished past a blemish,
could easily be Flemish.
Who has the time to find a rhyme
that works as hard as them-ish?

Gaze at the painting of George and the dragon.

The knight is dooming him at long lance.

Praise for the painting of George and the dragon.

The dragon is fuming with no second chance.

The damsel is praying her torment is through.

The dragon was preying too; it's what dragons do!

So goes the tale called the Golden Legend.

A girdle 'round the neck, and the beast was tame.

Thus ends the tale of Saint George and the Dragon.

England's patron saint lives on in fame.

*Saint George and the Dragon, c. 1438*, Martorell

*Mona Lisa*, Leonardo da Vinci

Really now, Leo,
what was your premise?
Is that a smile,
or is that a grimace?

Your chiaroscuro
is meant to obscure, no?

Is she that someone
you held dear, or
was it really you,
man, in the mirror?

I spotted *A Sunday Afternoon
　　　on the Island of La Grande Jatte*
from far across the room, and
　　　I liked it. I liked it a lot.
But, drawing closer to the scene
　　　by good Monsieur Seurat,
it appears that, when painting, he
　　　was merely connecting dot to dot.

*A Sunday Afternoon on the Island of La Grande Jatte*, Georges Seurat

*Self-Portrait in a Straw Hat*, Élisabeth Louise Vigée le Brun

Which was it—the hat
or for whom you sat—
that rendered you so coy?

You wear it (that smile)
avec plaisir, while
you turn me into your toy.

# Rodin Again

sung to "I'm Looking over a Four-Leaf Clover"

I sit and ponder,
"What's over yonder?
What am I missing here?"

I sit and ponder,
hunched in wonder,
chin on my fist, "Oh, dear . . ."

*Le Penseur/The Thinker*, Auguste Rodin

Sistine Chapel, Michelangelo

Ceiling painted lying down,
lying down,
lying down.
Four years flat upon his back,
Michelangelo.

Crowds of people looking up,
looking up,
looking up.
Crowds of people looking up
to Michelangelo.

Adam reaching with the stroke
of his hand,
Sistine man.
Fingers reach but never touch . . .
Michelangelo.

# Van Gogh, Going, Gone
sung to "Twinkle, Twinkle, Little Star"

Vincent painted *Starry Night*—
darkness filled with swirling light.
Heartaches haunted darker hours.
Brighter days brought *Sunflowers*.
Beauty lives, and art goes on—
Vincent van Gogh, going, gone.

*Vase with Twelve Sunflowers*, Vincent van Gogh

*Bend and Forest Road*, Cezanne

With cylinder, sphere, and cone,
he cut the image to the bone,
and next retraced
the hues—not space—
leaving "well enough" alone.

A perfect landscape frees
the forest from its trees.
He mapped relief
in bold belief:
Let green be green as it please!

Staying up late
at the café,
lonely nighthawks hang out there.
Do I gawk or glance or stare?
What's more proper,
Edward Hopper?

Looks so lonely:
colors only
show a darkened modern scene,
real as streets that look so lean—
isolation
of a nation.

*Nighthawks*, Edward Hopper

*Paris Street; Rainy Day*, Caillebotte

Caillebotte and cobblestones—
look at the sky, the sun is gone, and
even the tans are tinged with gray.
The word for the day is an umbrella.

Slow walk around the town,
don't let the grayness get you down.
Look to the left, or is that right?
They think you might need an umbrella.

La-da-da da-da da-da, an umbrella.
Do-do-do do-do you need an umbrella?

Sailing go the boats
    on a timeless sea.
Grains of sand
    slip through the hands:
    a lasting memory.

*Children Playing on the Beach*, Mary Cassatt

*The Elder Sister*, William Bouguereau

Bouguereau,
Bouguereau,
Bouguereau.
It's "follow the baby,
take care of the baby,
don't swallow the baby!
Watch after the baby."

"Let's coddle the baby."
It's "bottle for baby,"
then, "burp the baby."
(It's urp-ing, Oh, baby!)
Bouguereau,
Bouguereau,
Bouguereau.

Nee-ew diaper for baby.
Its butt feels like gravy!
My life is this baby.
I'm rife with this baby!

So, I'm thinking, maybe,
I'd rather catch rabies
than chase after babies!
It's driving me crazy!
Bouguereau,
Bouguereau,
Bouguereau.

So, rock-a-bye, baby,
go to sleep, little baby!
I'll lock away baby.
Not a peep from you, baby!

Don't smile at me, baby.
You're too cute, you baby.
I'll hold onto baby.
I'm sold on this baby!
Bouguereau,
Bouguereau,
Bouguereau.

# Degas Can-Can

sung to "The Can-Can"

Degas painted lots of dancers,
ballerina prancers
in the studio-io-io-i-uh-oh.

Liked to watch them dance en pointe:
unbent perfect joints
kept them on their toes-i-oes-i-oes-i-oh-no!

If he slipped off to the Moulin
Rouge to see the can-can,
it must not have impressed him much.

*Green Dancer*, Edgar Degas

*The Cardsharps*, Caravaggio

The cardsharps are cheating,
and it's so unfair.
That dupe is a loser
'cause he's unaware
the bloke in the cloak
is sneaking a peek.
When that six of clubs plays,
he'll read 'em and weep.

Notice the shadows,
the light and the dark.
That's chiaroscuro.
It's such a fine art.
A palette for fooling
conceals like a cloak.
The one holding the tray
is going baroque.

Elephants form swans in bogs.
Barren trees make upright logs.
Melting clocks run time agog.
Hello, Dalí.

*The Persistence of Memory*, Salvador Dalí

*The False Mirror*, Rene Magritte

Hello, big eyeball!
Come in my head, y'all,
window into my soul.
Pupil to sclera
looks like a mirror
turned upward to
a big sky of blue,
with clouds white as driven snow
Oh, brother!
What is up with my thought processor?

# Pop Goes the Warhol
sung to "Pop Goes the Weasel"

Classic artists painted gods
and sculpted all their heroes.
What do modern themes contain?
Pop goes the Warhol.

Quarter hours come and go
with soup cans for his models.
Fashions change, but time remains.
Pop goes the Warhol.

*Campbell's Soup Can*, Andy Warhol

*Flashlight III*, Jasper Johns

Jasper Johns,
Jasper Johns,
showed us coffee cans,
alphabets,
and painted flags
from waxy paper strands.
Oh!
Jasper Johns
framed ideas
everybody knows,
sculpting stuff
from every day—
like flashlights in repose.

Here's more than a sigh
      that meets the eye.
Did you have a bad dream?
Somebody dear to you tell you bye-bye?
I think I could cry.
Are you sad, or are you steamed?
Are you caught in a crunch?
Someone stole your lunch?
Let me guess—
      you were cut from the team.
No, wait, I know—
      your downloads won't stream!
Perhaps your pants have ripped a seam.
Or maybe you're trapped
inside a meme
the art critics deem
your signature theme.
Poor Mr. Munch.
You'll be remembered,
      it seems,
for one main idea—
      but,
Whoa!
It is quite a scream.

*The Scream*, Edvard Munch

*Convergence*, Jackson Pollock

Drippings and droppings
    and slingings of oil,
this way and that way
    in feverish toil.

Nonstrokes of genius
    all splattered around—
art and the eyes who behold
    are unbound.

The very idea!

To think that something—anything—

can mean more than it appears!

Each painting holds a brave new world inside its boundless frame.

The words we say say so much more than just what's in a name.

How, then, do we make sense of things?

    We smell the turf.

    We taste the surf.

    We hear a baby's cry.

    We reach beyond our very selves

        and touch an endless sky . . .

Do you begin to see it now—

how senses seam our seems?

This stuff we're made of is the stuff of everlasting dreams.

Pablo Picasso, *Woman in Hat and Fur Collar* (1937)
© 2020 Estate of Pablo Picasso / Artists Rights Society (ARS), New York

Frida Kahlo, *The Frame* (1938)
© 2020 Banco de México Diego Rivera Frida Kahlo Museums Trust, Mexico, D.F. / Artists Rights Society (ARS), New York

Georgia O'Keeffe, *Grey Line With Black, Blue And Yellow* (1923)
© 2020 Georgia O'Keeffe Museum / Artists Rights Society (ARS), New York

Grant Wood, *American Gothic* (1930)
© 2020 Figge Art Museum, successors to the Estate of Nan Wood Graham / Licensed by VAGA at Artists Rights Society (ARS), NY

Salvador Dalí, *The Persistence of Memory* (1931)
© 2020 Salvador Dalí, Fundació Gala-Salvador Dalí, Artists Rights Society

René Magritte, *The False Mirror* (1928)
© 2020 C. Herscovici / Artists Rights Society (ARS), New York

Andy Warhol, *Campbell's Soup Can* (Tomato Soup, 1964)
© 2020 The Andy Warhol Foundation for the Visual Arts, Inc. / Licensed by Artists Rights Society (ARS), New York

Jasper Johns, *The Flashlight III* (1958)
© 2020 Jasper Johns / Licensed by VAGA at Artists Rights Society (ARS), NY

Jackson Pollock, *Convergence* (1952)
© 2020 The Pollock-Krasner Foundation / Artists Rights Society (ARS), New York

hal evans believes travel is not complete without a visit to the local art museums. It is said that every picture tells a story. hal says that every picture tells many different stories—as many as the individuals who behold it. hal enjoys laughter. In addition to *ArtyFacts*, he has written humorous poetry, plays, prose, songs, and countless text messages.

hal has been known to play guitar, drums, tuba, and clarinet—though not all at the same time. He lives atop a mountain under a stream, inside a whisper, deep in a dream . . . and online at www.halevanspoet.com.